"ANSWERS FOR HUMANITIES QUEST FOR TRUTH"

"ANSWERS FOR HUMANITIES QUEST FOR TRUTH"

MICHELLE MATKO

XULON PRESS

Xulon Press
2301 Lucien Way #415
Maitland, FL 32751
407.339.4217
www.xulonpress.com

Unless otherwise indicated, Scripture quotations taken from the Amplified Bible (AMP). Copyright © 1954, 1958, 1962, 1964, 1965, 1987 by The Lockman Foundation. Used by permission. All rights reserved.

Paperback ISBN-13: 978-1-66286-779-8
Hard Cover ISBN-13: 978-1-66286-780-4
Ebook ISBN-13: 978-1-66286-781-1

PREFACE

I wrote this book because I wanted to share what I have found in my
quest for truth. In a world where there are so many opinions and life
circumstances, it's easy to get tossed like a wave on the ocean, leaving
you grasping for what is true. We may be told something is true, and
we may decide to believe it and make it our own truth, but often we are
deceived. My quest for truth began because I was told to believe certain
things and felt deceived. So I decided to dig deep into the Bible and get
God's truth, to fill myself up with the spirit of truth (the Holy Spirit) so
I would not believe or hold on to anymore lies. The following chapters
are filled with the truths I have found on my quest. I live these truths in
my everyday life. I hope and pray this book will be an inspiration and
a source of wisdom to all who read it and will help you to live, breathe,
and move in the spirit of truth!

TABLE OF CONTENTS

Chapter 1
I Am Yours and You Are Mine

After everything I have been through, when I hear you say this one thing to me, I realize nothing else really matters. It seems this is the very thing the enemy is always trying to take, who I am in you, who I belong to and who I stand for. This one truth will always remain, forever and ever and ever. Whether you say it to me, or I say it to you, my Daddy, my love, my friend, my savior, my healer—I am yours and you are mine. This one truth will keep all of us as your bride. We will be the beautiful bride prepared and made ready to see her king face to face one day very soon. No matter what goes on in this world, no matter what they say or do to us, we are here, nuzzled safe in the warmth of your heart and love for us. We cannot hear their lies, hate, or anger. All we hear is you. You give us truth, freedom, and safety within your refuge from all evil. It does not matter whether evil is spewed at our souls or our physical beings. In you we live, we breathe, and we have our being. We not only live, but we thrive; we not only thrive, but we are revived to revive others.

To say I am yours is to say you own me, you protect me. That means you protect everything concerning me, everything I hold dear to my heart, my loved ones, my land. To say that I am yours is to say my faith can only stay in that truth. That truth frees me from worry and doubt; it releases the tangible anointing to every situation that concerns me. That is why the devil is always attacking that truth. That truth causes me to remain in you and you in me, and there the devil cannot stop me from manifesting you on this earth and saving the lost from his grip. To say you are mine means that I take on your heart, love, and compassion. Not only do I take on your heart, love, and compassion, but your anointing belongs to me to disperse, to look for and save the lost, to be able to stand against evil and destruction. And on this earth, I can be your hands, feet, and mouthpiece to release your power on this earth. And as your people all do this in unity, we will see the knowledge of your glory fill this earth just as waters cover the sea!

My Beloved is mine and I am His, He pastures his flock among the lilies (Song of Sol. 2:16).

But the time is coming when the earth shall be filled with the knowledge of the glory of the Lord, as the waters cover the sea (Hab. 2:14).

Chapter 2

DEVIL, YOU ALREADY LOST

Devil, you already lost. Jesus defeated you thousands of years ago. He took the keys to hell and death and gave those keys to us. We let loose the power of God by the wind of the Holy Spirit against every scheme and plot. We bind you and annihilate your demonic stronghold. We rebuke you in the name of Jesus, and we stand in the victory of the Lord.

I have nothing else to say to that defeated foe, because the Word of God says on the last day, the nations will see how the devil is nothing but a powerless worm in comparison to the power, love, and deliverance of the Most High God. God gave us his Word that says He already won. Revelation 5:5 says, Fear not weep not; the Lion of the tribe of Judah has already triumphed. He is the author and the finisher! He is able to open the scroll and the seven seals. As we absorb that truth into our innermost being and praise Judah, victory shall go forth. Even amid our warfare, we take that wind of the Holy Spirit to the finish line of whatever we are facing. This will be an everyday occurrence for warriors in the kingdom. God tells us to be vigilant, awake, and alert. The devil's time is short, and he knows it, and he hates us. But greater is He that is in us than he that is in this world.

There is power in unity. That is why it's so vital that the message of victory over the devil is taught in these last days. At the same time that we battle in spiritual warfare in the last days, there will be a revealing of God's love and power on this earth. He will show with signs, wonders, and miracles that He is the Prince of Peace. Real peace, a peace that overcomes any devil in hell that comes to steal our peace. He alone is our defender!

I am the ever-living one, living in and beyond all space and time. I died, but see, I am alive forevermore, and I have the keys of absolute control and victory over death and of hades, the realm of the dead (Rev. 1:18). I will give you the keys [authority] of the kingdom of heaven, and whatever you bind, forbid, declare to be improper and unlawful on the earth will have already been bound in heaven, and whatever you loose, permit, declare lawful on the earth will have already been loosed in heaven (Matt. 16:19). Therefore rejoice, O heavens and earth and sea, because the devil has come down to you in great wrath, knowing that he has only a short time remaining (Rev. 12:12). Little children, believers, dear ones, you are of God and you belong to Him and have already overcome them, the agents of the antichrist, because He who is in you is greater than he [Satan] who is in the world of sinful mankind (1 John 4:4). These signs will accompany those who have believed: in My name they will cast out demons, they will speak in new tongues, they will pick up serpents, and if they drink anything deadly, it will not hurt them: they will lay hands on the sick, and they will get well (Mark 16:16–17).

Chapter 3
You Are a Father to the Fatherless

I will never forget when you started revealing your love to me. You are steadfast, always there. You are the same yesterday, today, and forever. Your word is Word; it is not shifty or deceptive. There are no ulterior motives with you. You are straight-up love. Your yes is yes, and your no is no. You do not want anything from me except my love because you loved me from my mother's womb before I took my first breath.

When my biological father was beating my mother's womb to kill me, because he did not want me, and my mother was hemorrhaging without stop, you were speaking the living Word that I was special. You are the one in Ezekiel that found me in my prenatal state after I was abused and abandoned by my biological father. Leaving us no choice but to run, you found me and restored me, you gifted me and favored me, you blessed me and covered me. I am yours and you are mine forever. I went on a quest to know you because you went on a quest to find me and keep me. In my knowing you, I discovered you want to support me. Everything I ask for, you say you want me to have because you trust me, knowing I am so in love with you because you alone are a good Father.

I believed you when you told me I am special and have a special purpose on this earth because you said before Jesus comes again, the spirit of Elijah must come. And this is my true passion, to reveal to this world that you are a good Father and have all the power to display you are good before all the false gods. To let the world know that you love us so much and have given us the power against terror, destruction, and a spirit of fear that leads to slavery. As we remember deliverance from bad fathers and hard task masters at Passover, we set the table and wait for the spirit of Elijah to open the door. The spirit of Elijah turns the hearts of fathers to the children, and the unscrupulous to the wisdom of the upright. We thank you, Abba, for your Father's love and for teaching us your ways!

When fathers are not present physically or spiritually with their families and have their minds set on their own pride and greed, and their own agenda on this earth, they display passive or open anger. They discipline their children in anger or pride instead of love. Disciplining in anger only produces fear and a broken spirit, not a willingness to be obedient. Disciplining in love produces wholeness.

Fathers like that seem to gloat and take pride in the brokenness and dysfunction of their children. They don't take the responsibility of being a father. They had dysfunction in their childhoods and now they take that dysfunction out on their kids and the mother of their children and then blame them for continued dysfunction, instead of apologizing and doing what is right to bring healing. Many times, they do not support their own flesh and blood. When fathers are not taking responsibility as fathers but trying to get everyone else to take their monetary responsibility, including the government, or manipulate systems and people based on only self, they betray the innocent. A father's heart must be one in God's heart first and foremost so they will manifest His heart and reveal the true Father God to their children.

We live in a world where even spiritual fathers have gotten away from your ways, God. The fathers of the church have even molested their spiritual children in many ways, by trying to control and keep them basically as slaves. They fear a lack of finances (even when they are wealthy themselves). Many are not allowing their congregation to flow in their gifts. They fear they are more anointed and they are not confident in their own gifts. Often times they suppress the gifts of the spirit in those God has chosen to serve along side of them because they are jealous or in competion, when they should trust the Holy Spirit to open up and allow the body to flow in their gifts and calling, so the church will be jointly fit with every part of the body fulfilling it's purpose and call. They don't understand the working of the gifts in unity and freedom of the Holy Spirit under the leading of the spiritual Father. Many of them do not even know they are in fear because of the tradition of the church they were trained or brought up in.

This tradition is what holds back the power of God, the Word says. And that power is the spirit of Elijah that will produce a true revival, not only in the church so that it will be awake and thriving, but it will awaken this world and reveal God's goodness and omnipotent power on this earth to save the lost in these last days. This is changing! The spirit of Elijah is being restored to God's people in these last days because Jesus is coming for us. We are making ready the way for Jesus to come.

You, Abba, are always doing things steadily, and always in truth. That is why I trust you, Abba. That is why I am called to fulfill a special purpose on this earth to confront these injustices and reveal the heart of our Father God, because it is not too late for fathers to turn to God's ways of wisdom. The door is open, and the table is set! Thankful for the Fathers including my own Dad, that are leading and flowing in the spirit of Elijah and are sitting at the table and have set the place of Elijah for all the fathers yet to come to the banqueting table!

Jesus Christ is eternally changeless, always the same, yesterday and today and forever (Heb. 13:8). James 1:17 says that every good thing given, and every perfect gift is from above; it comes down from the Father of Lights [the creator and sustainer of the heavens], in whom there is no variation or shadow of turning. He is perfect and never changes (Ps. 139:13–14). For you created my inmost being; you knit me together in my mother's womb. I praise you because I am fearfully and wonderfully made: your works are wonderful; I know that full well (Ezek. 16:6–14). And when I passed by you and saw you rolling about in your blood, I said to you in your blood, LIVE! Yes, I said to you still in your natal blood, LIVE! I caused you [Israel] to multiply as the bud which grows in the field, and you increased and became tall and you came to full maiden-hood and beauty: your breasts were formed and your hair had grown, yet you were naked and bare. Now I passed by you again and looked upon you: behold, you were maturing and at the time for love, and I spread My skirt over you and covered your nakedness. Yes, I plighted My troth to you and entered into covenant with you, says the Lord, and you became Mine. Then I washed you with water: yes, I thoroughly washed away your clinging blood from you and I anointed you with oil. I clothed you also with embroidered cloth and shod you with (fine seal) leather: and I girded you about with fine linen and covered you with silk. I decked you also with ornaments and I put bracelets on your wrists and a chain on your neck. I put a ring on your nostril and earrings in your ears and a beautiful crown upon your head! Thus, you were decked with gold and silver, and your raiment was of fine linen and silk and embroidered cloth: you ate fine flour and honey and oil. And you were exceedingly beautiful, and you prospered into royal estate. And your renown went forth among the nations for your beauty, for it was perfect through My majesty and splendor which I had put upon you, says the Lord God (Luke 1:17). And He Himself will go before Him [Christ's return] in the spirit of Elijah, to turn back the hearts of the fathers to the children, and the disobedient and incredulous and unpersuadable to the wisdom of the upright [which is the knowledge and holy love of the will of God] in order to make ready for the Lord a people perfectly prepared in spirit, adjusted, and disposed and placed in the right moral state (Eph. 6:4). Fathers, do not provoke your children to anger [do not exasperate them to the point of resentment with demands that are trivial, unreasonable, humiliating, or abusive: nor by showing favoritism or indifference to any of them] but bring them up tenderly with lovingkindness in the discipline and instruction of the Lord (1 Tim. 5:8). If anyone does not support his own, and especially for those of his own family, he has denied the faith [by disregarding its precepts] and is worse than an unbeliever [who fulfills his obligation in these matters].

Chapter 4

OUR HEART IS THE BREEDING GROUND

Create in me a clean heart; restore unto me the joy of my salvation. Take not thy holy spirit from me. As King David said to you, God, we say repeatedly. Cleanse, purify, and keep our hearts in you, Lord. Let my heart never be the experimental lab where people of all social classes try to make me see things their way, instead of your way. Let my heart not be a home for anyone that is not one with you. Keep my heart tender, with the soil stirred up soft, so when the seed of your living word is planted, it will spring up a beautiful harvest. Living manna that will sustain many, as a generous crop coming from the depths of my heart. As a beautiful garden that bears your intricate creativity, budding forth the salvation for all that I meet, or that see my life. Fill me so I follow you and produce you from the depths of my being. Water my spirit and inner man in the depths of my heart with your raining living waters so I am planted by streams with a continual supply and everything I do comes to completion. Let my roots go down deep so when the winds of adversity and winds of doctrine and opinions of people, governments, and systems blow, I am not uprooted from your truth and steadfast love.

Let me count the cost of building the kingdom and be willing to sacrifice my heart for others as an offering poured out, with the understanding that you will keep filling it with joy, knowing the harvest of my heart will be the salvation for their hearts from the sacrificial offering of mine. Let me never forget that I am the keeper and guard of my heart. That what I allow into it is what will be the issues that flow from it.

Let my heart continually produce and multiply you and you alone, my Abba. Let the brightness of your glory shine deep into my innermost being so it causes me to arise and spring forth glory unto your name. Let me always stay tender and open to receive your word, keep the living streams of your word flowing brighter and brighter as I continually pour out your prophetic word and truths, risking all while guarding your word, and those you have entrusted me to reach. Let me be whole and fully rounded in your truth and ways that you will always have my heart and no devil in hell will be able to steal what you have planted in me. I have your heart and You have mine! (Ps. 51:10–11)

Create in me a clean heart, Oh God, and renew a right and steadfast spirit within me. Do not cast me away from your presence and do not take your Holy Spirit from me (Ps. 1:1).

Blessed, fortunate, prosperous, and favored by God is the man who does not walk in the counsel of the wicked [following their advice and example], nor stand in the path of sinners, nor sit [down to rest] in the seat of scoffers [ridiculers]. But his delight is in the law of the Lord, and His law. In His precepts and teachings he habitually meditates day and night. And he will be like a tree firmly planted and fed by streams of water which yields its fruit in its season and its leaf does not fade. And in whatever he does, he prospers and comes maturity. For who, when he wants to build a watchtower [for his guards] does not first sit down and calculate the cost, to see if he has enough to finish it (Luke 14:28).

Watch over your heart with all diligence, for from it flow the springs of life (Prov. 4:23).

Chapter 5
THE SAME POWER IN GOD'S MOUTH IS IN OUR MOUTHS

The whole earth was filled with darkness and God said Let there be light and there was light. In Hebrews we read that the earth was created and spoken into being by faith. When God speaks, His word is omnipotent, all powerful. There is no force in darkness that overcomes it; His word overcomes.

When we become born again and filled with the Holy Spirit and speak His word, the same word of God that was in Jesus's mouth is now in our mouths. It is omniscient, full of complete wisdom and insight. He knows exactly what we need, when and how. He is omnipresent. As we speak and say what He says, it is sent throughout space and time right to the point of need. It is alive, it is penetrating, and it cannot be stopped. It is sharper than any two-edged sword, dividing and cutting through a person between soul and spirit, right to the heart, to the point of need. Examine the motive of the heart, so we will be a people aligned to receive all that God wants to do in and through us through His living word. The living word is a seed that is planted in our hearts. If the soil is tender, pure, and cared for, as I wrote in the earlier chapter, it will surely spring forth into a great harvest. If it is rejected, the word has still gone forth and done its job, so all men will be without excuse on the last day at the Bema Seat of God. He is a God of justice.

As we pray in the power of the Holy Spirit, being Holy Spirit led, we are releasing His omnipotent power right to the point of need to carry out exactly what is in His heart and mind to do in us and through us on this earth.

I believe one of the greatest truths that can be understood is the power of His word, but to release and manifest His word you must know His word, by reading and studying His written word—the Bible. This will teach you His heart and character. This comes from spending time with Him, reading His word and praying, and understanding He is a person. He made us in His image to create, to love, to defend, and to overcome. He made us to be fruitful and multiply. Everything He made multiplies. Everything He made is good.

Two different people can speak the same scripture out of the Bible, but in one person's mouth it is released in the atmosphere by faith. The Bible tells us that faith cometh by hearing, and hearing by the word of God. That is, a person that has come to know the heart and character of God and spent time in His presence and studying His word to know His character and believes He will do what He says. He is not a man that would lie to us, but He is true to His word.

The word will never return void. In the other person's mouth, without faith, the Bible says we cannot even please God. We must believe that He is God, and He is a rewarder of those that diligently seek Him out. The Bible says to ask for the Holy Spirit and the gifts of the spirit.

Every born-again, spirit-filled child of God can speak the written Logos word of God and see it become Ramah (living, active) and come to fruition to any situation that it pertains to and is spoken to. But then many are given the gift of prophecy. The word says that God wishes all prophesy, so ask! It is a gift of the Holy Spirit used for edification, exhortation, and revealing the will and purpose of God by speaking His word into a situation. Then some are called to the office of the prophet to speak on behalf of God, many times speaking the word of God from His heart on matters in the nations, governments, systems, churches, and with individuals. It is not only a gift, but an umbrella of many gifts and an election of God's will for a person's life to stand for Him, His government (kingdom), and His heart and will in regard to the root of a matter that needs to be confronted and changed. It is so that man has an opportunity to repent and will be without excuse on the last day of the judgment seat of God. Many times, the heart of God is spoken, and His goodness and power are poured out by His living prophetic word, as a literal move of God to bring an awakening and revolution to nations, governments, systems, churches, and individuals. The word says that we prophesy according to the measure of our faith, so it is so vital to stay in the word since that is how our faith is built and we then have faith in God to perform His word, so we are willing to risk it and step out and say what He is saying because we know he will back His own word! In the beginning God [Elohim] created by forming from nothing the heavens and the earth. The earth was formless and void or a waste and emptiness, and darkness was upon the face of the deep [primeval ocean that covered the unformed earth]. The spirit of God moving [hovering, brooding] over the face of the waters and God said, "Let there be light" and there was light (Gen. 1:1–3).

In the beginning before all time was the word Christ and the Word was with God, and the Word was God Himself. He was continually existing in the beginning co-eternally with God. All things were made and came into existence through Him and without Him not even one thing was made that has come into being. In Him was life and the power to bestow life and the life was the Light of men (John 1:1–5). Since we have gifts that differ according to the grace given to us, each of us is to use them accordingly: if someone has a gift of prophesy, let him speak a new message from God to His people in proportion to the faith possessed

(Rom. 12:6). By faith [that is, with an inherent trust and enduring confidence in the power, wisdom, and goodness of God] we understand that the worlds [universe, ages] were framed and created [formed, put in order, and equipped for their intended purpose] by the word of God so that what is seen was not made out of things which are visible (Heb. 11:3). For the word of God is living and active and full of power [making it operative energizing and effective]. It is sharper than any two-edged sword, penetrating as far as the division of the soul and the spirit [the completeness of a person] and of both joints and marrow [the deepest parts of our nature] exposing and judging the very thoughts and intentions of the heart (Heb. 4:12). And He when He comes, will convict the world about the guilt of sin and the need for a savior and about righteousness and about judgement (John 16:8). In the same way the spirit comes to us and helps us in our weakness. We do not know what prayer to offer or how to offer it as we should, but the spirit Himself (knows our need and at the right time) intercedes on our behalf with sighs and groanings too deep for words (Rom. 8:26). God is not a man, that He should lie, nor a son of man, that He should repent. Has He said, and will He not do it? Or has He spoken, and will He not make it good and fulfill it? (Num. 23:19) So will My word be which goes out of My mouth: It will not return to Me void (useless, without result), without accomplishing what I desire, and without succeeding in the matter for which I sent it (Isa. 55:11). But without faith it is impossible to walk with God and please Him, for whoever comes near to God must necessarily believe that God exists and that He rewards those who earnestly and diligently seek Him (Heb. 11:6). If you, then being evil that is, sinful by nature, know how to give good gifts to your children, how much more will your heavenly Father give the Holy Spirit to those who ask and continue to ask Him! (Luke 11:13) Pursue this love with eagerness, make it your goal, yet earnestly desire and cultivate the spiritual gifts to be used by believers for the benefit of the church, but especially that you may prophesy to fore-tell the future, to speak a new message from God to the People. For the one who speaks in an unknown tongue does not speak to people but to God: for no one understands him or catches his meaning, but by the spirit he speaks mysteries, secret truths, hidden things. But on the other hand, the one who prophesies speaks to people for edification to promote their spiritual growth and speak words of encouragement to uphold and advise them concerning matters of God and speaks words of consolation to compassionately comfort them. One who speaks in a tongue edifies himself, but one who prophesies edifies the church, promotes growth in spiritual wisdom, devotion, holiness, and joy). Now I wish that all of you spoke in unknown tongues, but even more I wish that you would prophesy. The one who prophesies is greater and more useful than the one who speaks in tongues, unless he translates and explains what he says, so that the church may be edified [instructed, improved, strengthened] (I Cor. 14:1). Now the Word of the Lord came to me saying, Before I formed you in the womb, I knew you and approved of you as My chosen instrument, And before you were born I consecrated you [to Myself as My own]: I have appointed you as a prophet to the nations (Jer. 1:4). Then the Lord stretched out His hand and touched my mouth and the Lord said to me "Behold [hear me] I have put My words in your mouth. See I have appointed you this day over the nations and over the kingdoms, to uproot and break down, to destroy and overthrow, to build and to plant" (Jer. 1:9.)

Chapter 6

WE ARE EMPTIED TO BE FILLED AND USED

A truth that is so profound and the most fulfilling thing that we can do is to say, "Less of me and more of you, God." When we purposefully empty ourselves and say, "Fill me, God, with all of you. Not my will, but your will be done," we are open, we are receptive, we are willing, obedient, and humble. We know we can do nothing in our own strength, but every good and perfect gift comes from Him. In our very weakness, His power is made strong. The Word says He will take the weak and foolish things of this world to confound the wise. Because the ones that no one would pick are usually the ones that God picks, that know we can do nothing, but God can do all things. That is the danger in these last days, that man is so filled with pomp of his own accomplishments that he feels he has no need for God. He cannot take one trophy, certificate, degree, title, or bank account to heaven or hell when he goes. We can move all of heaven with the heart cry, "Daddy, I need you!" God stands up at the sound of our voice and all the angel armies of heaven come to our rescue. It is in that place of "I need you, God; I know I cannot do this on my own." God loves to be our deliverer and savior. It is who He is, His very character. He promises not to fail us.

The man that does things in his own strength and takes all the credit has already received his reward on earth, the Bible says. That is all he gets, and that is why he is never satisfied. Because anything that does not last eternally does not satisfy. It is temporal, and man innately knows it, whether he admits it or not. He is longing for the eternal, for eternal life, to live forever with the King of all Kings in a kingdom that does not end. He is longing for the reward that comes from God and lasts forever. Man is longing for God's love, and if he does not get it, he looks for it in all the wrong places, often in his own accomplishments and has become a god unto himself. Everybody is made to worship God, and so that innate desire to worship will worship something, even himself if he is not worshipping God. What he does not realize is he cannot save himself from hell. He cannot speak to the wind and waves and cause a storm to be thwarted and the sun to come out supernaturally. Or command a flood to dissipate or for the clouds to open in a deluge to satisfy a drought. He cannot still an earthquake or send angels to overcome a terrorist in his own voice. When given a report from the doctor with no hope, he cannot live.

But filled with the overflowing power of the Holy Spirit, emptied of anything except God and a desire to please Him, we can move mountains, thwart storms, satisfy droughts, plead mercy over cities, be healed and heal the sick with or without any help from man, medicine, or natural resources. We can stand against terror and call the angel armies of heaven in our defense in only the name of the Most High God! Not in our name, not in our strength. Man does not have the supernatural qualities to change an effect in nature and the natural elements. But filled with the Holy Spirit, speaking the Word of God in faith, in God and God alone, absolutely nothing is impossible! We have the authority to speak to and tear down powers and principalities of darkness and wickedness in high places. When we are emptied of everything contrary to God and His ways, filled with all of God and his power from on high, we then rise supernaturally in victory in any area of life and warfare.

Jesus said, "Take up your cross daily and follow me, in living and in dying if necessary." It is all about His will and purpose. All about glorifying Him on this earth so that all will come to the saving knowledge of who He is. I have been crucified with Christ [that is, in Him I have shared His crucifixion], it is no longer I who live, but Christ lives in me. The life I now live in the body I live by faith, by adhering to, relying on, and completely trusting in the Son of God, who loved me and gave Himself up for me (Gal. 2:20). Then you will call on Me and you will come and pray to Me, and I will hear your voice and I will listen to you. Then with a deep longing, you will seek Me and require Me as a vital necessity, and you will find Me when you search for Me with all your heart (Jer. 29:12–13). For the weapons of our warfare are not carnal but might in God for pulling down strongholds, casting down arguments and every high thing that exalts itself against the knowledge of God, bringing every thought into captivity to the obedience of Christ (2 Cor. 10:4).

Chapter 7

GOD CONFIRMS HIS WORD WITH TWO TO THREE WITNESSES

An amazing Truth that brings such confidence when ministering the Word of God and knowing that God is with us, especially when being persecuted because of the Word, is that God backs His Word with two to three witnesses. The Bible says if we believe, signs, wonders, and miracles will follow. If God sends a prophet to speak over your life or into a situation, it is confirmed by what they said when it happens and manifests. It's undeniable that God spoke. He will often send another prophet to confirm the same word, or you will open the Bible and the written word will become Ramah and confirm the spoken word of prophecy or vice versa, even before the prophetic Word of God manifests. This has worked very strongly in my life.

I believe because of the platform I am on, that causes such persecution because of the manifestation of God's Word, that that has undeniably shown God to be God, and His character proven as a good Father that saves, delivers, and restores. That victory is in Him and Him alone. No idol or man can take His glory. It only belongs to Him and has been shown in real time with signs, wonders, and miracles. No devil in hell can perform or explain the manifested signs, wonders, and miracles of God because they are all good. The devil comes to rob, kill, and destroy. But Jesus came to give life and life abundantly. The devil has lost. His false accusations are proven false because all the good miracles manifested after the prophetic Word of God was spoken against, storms, floods, earthquakes, terror, and disease. Jesus said evil would not overtake evil. In the supernatural realm, only God can overtake evil. The devil would not overtake his own kingdom. Why would he defeat himself?

Common sense says a prophet or man would not risk his life to do good and save others from destruction unless he is good. This was the very accusation they used against Jesus when he was going about doing good everywhere he went. Regardless of what anyone thought of Him or said about Him, Jesus said if they did this to him, they would do it to us. So, we must, like him, manifest and not hold back the goodness of God on this earth, and risk our lives for His sake. We will overcome by the blood of the lamb and the word of our testimony, despite the persecution. He will do this by confirming the Word with two to three witnesses to show that He is with us. He will literally cause His people to become a wonder on the earth and make history. Jesus will be lifted up so that all men will be drawn to Him. Whether they receive him or not when they are drawn will be the choice of their own free will. But we as His people will have done all that we could have done in the power of His might to save them. And our reward will be great. He is our great reward! And I, if and when I am lifted up from the earth on the cross, will draw all people to Myself [Gentiles, as well as Jews] (John 12:32–34).

But He said to me, "My grace is sufficient for you, my lovingkindness and my mercy are more than enough—always available—regardless of the situation. For my power is being perfected and is completed and shows itself most effectively in your weakness. Therefore, I will even more gladly boast in my weaknesses, so that the power of Christ may completely enfold me and may dwell in me (2 Cor. 12:9).

God has selected for his purpose the foolish things of the world to shame the wise (revealing their ignorance, and God has selected for His purpose the weak things of the world to shame the things which are strong [revealing their fragility], God has selected for His purpose the insignificant [base] things of the world, and the things that are despised and treated with contempt, even the things that are nothing, so that He might reduce to nothing the things that are, so that no one may be able to boast in the presence of God (1 Cor. 1:27–29). He must increase in prominence, but I must decrease (John 3:30–32). This is the third time that I am visiting you. Every fact shall be sustained and confirmed by the testimony of two or three witnesses (2 Cor. 13:13). Look to Me and be saved; all the ends of the earth! For I am God, and there is no other. I have sworn by Myself; the word is gone out of My mouth in righteousness and shall not return, that unto Me every knee shall bow, and every tongue shall swear allegiance. Only in the Lord shall one say, I have righteousness [salvation and victory] and strength to achieve (Isa. 45:22–24).

The thief comes only to steal and kill and destroy. I came that they may have life, and have it in abundance to the full, till it overflows (John 10:10). When His own family heard this they went to take custody of Him: for they were saying, "He is out of His mind." The scribes who came down from Jerusalem were saying "He is possessed by Satan and He is driving out demons by the power of the ruler of demons" So He called them to Himself and spoke to them in parables. How can Satan drive out Satan? (Mark 3:21) And they went out and preached everywhere, while the Lord was working with them and confirming the word by the signs that followed (Mark 16:20).

Chapter 8

GOD IS LOVE

When I was a little girl, I did not believe that people loved me even if they said they did. After having my biological father play with our minds, beat my mother in front of us, keep things like water from us even when we were crying for it, and then pretend he was going to give it to us but never would and then would laugh at our pain. He would then act like we were the ones that were bad. Nothing was good enough for him. I did not trust because every time I thought I would step out and trust him, he would prove that he could not be trusted. This type of behavior makes a person feel like they are not worthy of love, like they are bad and do not deserve it. A child that has been molested or taken advantage of in any way bears the shame of it, believing it is their fault and they are the ones that are bad. The sad truth is that in this world there is so much dysfunction, selfishness, and greed.

Many men control to feel like they are a man. Relationships end up in divorce, many times without true reconciliation because of pride. People would rather stay in denial or lie about their behavior and misdeeds than to repent. Many men treat women as only an object for their use, instead of a loving help mate that has been made to satisfy and complete their lives. This is not love; it is using a person of value for selfish needs. This must change, and thank God it is changing. In a loving Godly covenant relationship, all those needs are met in love, heart to heart, and not for a superficial surface purpose out of fleshly dictates for self.

I have made it my quest to teach and show the ways of God and His goodness and His manifested power so that this will change. Instead of trying to change a man to bring closure to this pain I feel when I recognize by the spirit a lack of love and dysfunction, it has become my primary purpose to reveal God's love to the world, because I know all too well how the lack of it destroys lives. We must know our own identity and value so we will love ourselves and value ourselves to guard our hearts. No matter how much we want to help someone change, we cannot. Only God can change this lack of love in people, churches, and governments. No matter how nice and good we are, they will continue in their lies and controlling behaviors because of pride.

We can prove the love of God and reveal it so people will repent. There is hope for a lost and hurting world. It is God. But even God cannot change a person that does not want to change. They must repent and want to know God and His love and allow Him to fill them with His love. The Bible says He works in love and displays love and has a strong emotion of love for us. The definition of God is love. A person, church, or government that knows and works in the love of God will produce a bond of covenant, not control that leads to slavery based out of fear. A spirit of love is the Abba daddy kind of love. Abba daddy's love is solid, trustworthy, two-sided. Not a dominating side, but mutual admiration and respect. Many times, it is one-sided in the beginning of a relationship, until love wins and covenant is made. Real covenant is two-sided. All that I am is yours, and all you are is mine. I will fight for you, protect you, and give all for you. I went on a quest to find out the character of God and who He is and what love is. I learned some important truths to know, teach, and show right out of the Word of God, where my quest was satisfied, and my questions were answered many years ago. First, love never fails. So, to win at life, in relationships, in dealings in government, to have a successful business or anything we put our hand to, we must have love. We must have God. He did it all for us because He is love. If He did that for us, we must know there is nothing else He cannot do because His love is greater than anything on this earth that would rob, kill, and destroy us. It says in 1 Corinthians 13 that love is kind. If love is kind, that must mean God is not mean. It says love is patient and long suffering. So that means God will lovingly meet each person where they are, and even if they seem like they are rejecting Him, He is patient and in pursuit of their heart so they can know His love, the only hope that never fails. Love always considers someone else before they consider themselves.

Jesus said there was no greater love than to lay down your life for one another. We are willing to risk our lives and take the way of the cross to save others and reveal His love. We know it is the only answer.

Love does not let the devil win; we forgive people that mistreat us and teach them the love of God. But love is Justice. It defends and loves the oppressed so much as to deliver from evil. Love hates wrong and injustice, because love loves people so much it will risk its own life to save the innocent and oppressed. It will speak against evil out of love.

The Bible tells us to put on love as we would a garment. That means it is intentional. In any relationship, marriage, friendship, business, even government. We put it on as one in marriage, as one nation under God. Having one heart, mind, and purpose in God's love, no matter what we face, we intentionally clothe ourselves with His love. He is all that we need. He covers us and keeps us in His loving care. On the battlefield it is our armor. In the arms of our mate, it is the greatest comfort for our physical bodies. Love is not only spiritual, but manifested in our natural needs and circumstances. Husbands, love your wives, just as Christ also loved the church and gave Himself up for her (Eph. 5:25). The one who does not love has not become acquainted with God [does not and never did know Him] For God is love (1 John 4:8). (He is the originator of love, and it is an enduring attribute of His nature.) For you have not received a spirit of slavery leading again to fear [of God's judgement], but you have received the spirit of adoption as sons [the spirit producing sonship] by which we joyfully cry "Abba Father"! (Rom. 8:15) God loved the world so much that He gave His only son, that whoever would believe in Him would not perish but have eternal life. He won over hell and death (John 3:16). NO one has greater love [nor stronger commitment] than to lay down his own life for his friends (John 15:13). And above all these, put-on love and enfold yourselves with the bond of perfectness [which binds everything together completely in ideal harmony] (Col. 3:14).

Chapter 9

ONE PERSON CAN MAKE A DIFFERENCE

In the Word, Matthew 9:20, we see that there was one woman with an issue of blood. She had already sought out all that humanity and this world had to offer as a solution to her need. Nothing helped; nothing money could buy in this world sufficed. Man had failed her. She needed real power, God's power. This realization caused her to press past the crowd to touch Jesus. He stopped in His tracks and said, "I felt power release and flow out of my body. Who touched me?" The Word says in 2 Chronicles 16:9 that the Eyes of the Lord roam back and forth on this whole earth looking for just even one person that he can show himself strong. The truth and reality of these passages of scriptures shows us that one person on the whole earth, one person in a group of people. One person in the nation, one person, just one little girl or boy, man or woman. One businessperson, one politician, one movie star, one orphan, one soldier, one homemaker. One inner-city child, one grandma, one pastor, one prophet, one evangelist, one songwriter, one ballplayer, one cop or special agent, one warrior, one deaf or blind child, one sick person on their deathbed, one apostle, one teacher, one slave, one nobody in the world's lowest opinion, or greatest in the estimation of men, can get the attention of God Himself. The devil is always after this one truth. He does not want us to believe it. He hits us with accusations of, who do we think we are? How dare you think it was you that got God's attention. There are many people praying. Who are you compared to them? If we believe his lie, the storm would have hit, the earthquake would have destroyed, the nation would have been hit again. One voice can and does make a difference!

You can make a difference. If every person thought like that, got the attention of God, spoke out, and stepped out, the glory of God would manifest to such a degree that we would see the biggest move of God on this earth. We would make history. We would get the attention of the entire world and manifest His power as His children that it would cause even unbelievers to look. And so it will be, says the Lord!

It is a false humility to say that God cannot use one person to manifest the power of God in fullness, because it is the power of God and not our power. And that is true humility!

If we understand why the devil hates us, we will understand why we are so valuable. We are special. In Matthew 24:14, it says many are called but few are chosen, because few will raise their hand and reach past others to get to God, few will raise their hand and say, "Right here, God, use me! Choose me. Show yourself strong. Even if I am the only one, if all others run away in the face of persecution, I say yes, even if I must go alone, stand alone. I realize I am never alone; you are with me. And as I see in the spirit, there are more with us than against us." The responsibility is personal, and that is when we meditate on the truth that He can use just one person, and we surrender to that truth. As the gospel is preached and this truth is made known, we will come together as one body, one heart, and one mind. We must pray with the tenacity that we are or may be the only one praying, as if it depends on us taking our responsibility. Since we all fulfill different parts of the body and have a special assignment, we will take our place and come together as one, jointly fit, and flowing God's power and goodness on this earth, everyone doing their part.

The woman needed Jesus and pressed past all the people that were complacent and felt like he would not notice them anyway. There was a desperate tenacity and belief that if she could just touch him, there would be deliverance. Deliverance that no man on this earth could bring. When the scripture tells us that God is looking for us, looking for a heart that is open and desperate for Him, this shows His desire to show Himself strong on our behalf. He is willing, and He is not only willing, He is able!

Instead of waiting on someone else to speak the truth, step out in faith. Don't compete with their ability and strength to receive a temporal reward and result. We are after His virtue, power, and strength to be released in and through us; we are desperate for Him! The heart that has got to have Him, the heart that says nothing else will do, only you, God, the heart that says I can't wait for anyone else to stand up, speak up, I have got to go, say, do, and be all that God has called me to be! Why? Because I must have something other than this world's system, deception, pride of man, and fear. I need you, God, to show up, show off, and take all the Glory! If you can use anything, use Me, God! Then a woman who had suffered from a hemorrhage for twelve years came up behind him and touched the tassel fringe of his outer robe, for she had been saying to herself, "If I only touch His outer robe, I will be healed." But Jesus turned and seeing her said, "Take courage, daughter: your personal trust and confident faith in me has made you well." And at once the woman was completely healed (Matt. 9:20–22).

Chapter 10
THE LEVEL OF DESIRE TO TOUCH LIVES = THE LEVEL OF MANIFESTED RESURRECTION POWER

I will never forget being in San Francisco about eighteen years ago. We were going to be there for a week or so, and the forecast for the whole week was rain. As a matter of fact, they had not seen the sun in a month or so. I remember praying and asking God for a miracle since I never got a chance to go anywhere special or take any kind of vacation. There was sunshine, bright sunshine, not a cloud in the sky the whole time we were there. Every day from the first day we got there until the day we left. And the bizarre thing is that the forecast never changed. The weather report was predicting rain in the 90 percent range every morning. I would listen to the weather report and even the meteorologists were dumbfounded. I remember being on a ferry and overhearing several people talking about it, locals saying they could not believe it, that it had been depressing how gray it had been for so long. And the fact that the weather kept forecasting rain and the sun was so bright that week, it was astounding. As soon as we left, it rained again.

I will never forget going all by myself out on a mountain there and overlooking the ocean and prophesying the Word of the Lord, that even as I saw him answer my simple prayer, I would see the masses according to my heart's desire be saved and know His saving lovingkindness to all who would believe. It was the most powerful word speaking of revival among all people, all levels of society, from the poor to the rich. Every culture and race. That the knowledge of the Glory of the Lord would fill the earth as waters cover the sea (Hab. 2:14).

I remember this deep longing, a frustration that I wanted everyone to know, I wanted to have a loudspeaker to tell the universe, not only the church, but the entire world. And just like my voice was resounding over the waters, God had said the start of a huge revival had started right there. To this day I am not sure if the revival started in me, and started there right then, or if it means I will be instrumental in a revival now that I finally moved to California. I do know the knowledge of the Glory of the Lord started to manifest in me with a desire that it would fill the earth in such a measure and has only increased, that I am in awe myself. I do know that my desire that all would know this act of God is not just a happenstance, luck, or a one-time chance phenomenon that happened. But this is my Good Daddy in heaven that I take at His word. The Word says we will do the works that Jesus did and greater.

Jesus spoke to the weather, and it did what He said literally. This miracle was the manifestation of the kingdom of heaven in and through one little girl inside a woman's body that wanted to have fun and enjoy herself and to live life according to His Word. I started going into malls and other places, and everywhere I went I wanted to tell people. I almost took a chair and stood on it in a mall once because I wanted to wake them all up. Everywhere I went I realized they did not know. They did not know God like I know God. They did not even ask Him or know to ask him. Some know He is God, but like nailing Jesus on the cross all over again, for whatever reason they will not let Him be God or believe that what He did to redeem humanity was enough. Or they do not even understand what being redeemed and the fullness of our redemption means. In John

14:14, Jesus said in the kingdom of God we are told to ask anything and everything and it shall be done, presenting all that Jesus is! Watching people suffer with sickness, when we all with childlike faith can pray, and when so many others do not even give God a fighting chance, I did, and I wanted them to, too! I only saw some in the church working in this kind of power. Some that I listened to, as they taught right from the Word, work in this kind of faith and manifested power. But not everyone in the church was doing this and certainly not the mass of people in the world. I wanted to touch them, not only reach the indigent and inner-city people, like I had spent so many years of my life doing, but to reach the rich and famous, reach the kings in the earthly kingdoms of this world. Those that thought money could buy everything they needed and had no need for God. I wanted to reveal His goodness through creation and reveal everything the blood redeemed us from and gave us power to.

The Bible says Jesus was moved with compassion for people, and it would cause Him to go about doing good, healing all, doing miracles everywhere he went. His one purpose was to reveal the Father and the Father's heart of love, and manifest that power of love on the earth.

I remember taking 4 a.m. walks in my neighborhood with the compassion and frustration of desire to wake everyone up to who God is. I wanted to reveal Him. Imagining all kinds of scenarios while I was walking and praying, to then be dreaming that I was surrounded by all the media and masses of people and God's victory was flowing in every area. Satisfying droughts, winning in every city, overcoming evil and terrorists. Crazy good dreams, surrounded by media, with my answer to them being, "It is all God, only Him, every victory, triumph, miracle is in God and God alone. Pointing all Glory to Him!"

In retrospect, just so no one could say that it was luck or chance what happened in San Francisco, My good Daddy let me pray against storms and take vacations with the same scenario as San Francisco, and He did the same thing, causing the sun to come out repeatedly on this network. This network that I dreamed about and am still not sure what it is. But no matter what man did to me, God has used it to reach people and save many people and reveal His heart. And as I clothe myself in love and praise to Him and Him alone and patiently look to Him and Him alone, He answers my every heart cry. He is so good, and He is so real. And He loves us so much. He hears us and is more real than any earthly report we could ever get. His kingdom is greater than this earthly world; it supersedes the natural. If we pray according to His will, whatever we ask is done. It is finding out what His will is. His will is good. Think what you would do for your child. If your kids want to have a nice week at the beach and to have fun, of course, you want that for them. So does your Daddy in heaven. If you would protect your friends and family from a bad man or terror, so would your Daddy in heaven. If you want your friends and family to be blessed and win the championship, so does your Daddy in heaven. He has already won over the devil. Bad is bad to God, and good is good. Part of the mandate and call of God on my life has been to reveal good Daddy versus bad Daddy, in other words God versus Satan, truth versus deception, life versus death.

A truth within this truth is realizing our confidence is not in ourselves or even our own faith, but in God. Our only confidence is in Him, because He loves us more than we will ever know until we see Him face to face one day. As we keep taking Him at His Word, he reveals that love to us in a greater measure every time we step out in faith. If it is God's will and His Word, He will do it. It is for His namesake. We are here to lift Him up so that all men are drawn unto Him.

The truth I have learned is the desperate heart cry in us is what moves our Daddy. Our simple confidence in His goodness moves all of heaven on our behalf. He loves it when we step out and He must back His Word. It shows we believe in Him and His goodness and love for us. And he loves that. He wants relationship with us, and it hurts His heart when we do not believe Him or trust Him or listen to Him. Like when we try to help someone and they will not receive it, it hurts. He made us in His image. We must understand He is the person of the Holy Spirit and made us to have a relationship with Him.

He is a Father to us. Jesus is our bridegroom. He gave it all for us. What more could He give? To not receive from Him is to say He is not enough, or He is not good, or He does not care. The truth must be told, He is more than enough, He is so good, and He cares more that we will ever know in our finite minds. Let us give Him a chance to be God and be all that He wants to be in our lives and on this earth! Take Him at His Word. Step out in faith!

If you know how much God loves you, you will let Him be God, you will understand His compassion is so great for you, His mercies are unfailing and are new every morning. His faithfulness is not dependent on us, but on who He is. The more we understand this truth, the more we will understand it is all in Him, the strength to achieve, victory, every good and perfect gift comes from Him! Let Him be God in your life and those you love and care for.

We cannot get disillusioned in challenging times of testing of our faith. We cannot measure whether something was God or not depending on how long it takes to manifest. Many people give up right before they break through. We must hold on to Him no matter what it looks like. The ultimate result will always be a miracle glorifying His name if we receive and take Him at His Word. Again I say to you, that if two believers on earth agree, that is, are of one mind, in harmony, about anything that they ask within the will of God, it will be done for them by My Father in heaven (Matt. 18:19).

When we study the Word in Hebrews 11, we see great men and women of old went through a process to the manifestation of the Word of

God. This is called the cross. Surrendering to God's will and Word when it is painful, and we look crazy for believing. Believing when we cannot see the miracle yet in the natural. Believing when we are being persecuted and mocked for our faith. Whether it is a quick manifestation of His Word or we receive through patience, there is always the way of the cross. There was a category 5 hurricane headed straight for us in Tampa, Florida. Schools were shut down, and it started getting scary in the atmosphere. Fear was hitting everyone; store lines were long with buyers getting water and candles. I looked like a crazy person as I was walking around outside declaring and decreeing God's Word that it would not hit us, that His Word shall be done! I surely had at least one person listening to me that agreed against the coming destruction. And if not, I had the person of the Holy Spirit, the spirit of truth in agreement. and that was my only confession and stance in the middle of fear and panic. The eerie feeling when everything is gray and all the water and batteries are sold out in every store and lines are long with everyone stalking up on dry goods and candles. People were lined up filling up their gas tanks and driving in the opposite direction of where the path of storm was heading, which was straight toward us! Yet, my only confession was, it shall be done, I agree with the word that we can speak to wind and waves and do the work that Jesus did as He said, "Ask anything and everything and it shall be done!" Within that day, while the doppler was still showing it was coming straight for us, people were mocking me. That is called the cross. We hold on, we cannot do anything but trust and look to Him and take Him at His Word. That is our confidence. The storm never hit! I have spoken dissipation or that a storm would turn away again and again and again as hurricanes and tropical storms formed and threatened my friends and family, and time and time again the wind and waves obeyed at the Word of the Lord. It is God's Word to us. I once gave a tropical storm twenty-four hours to get out of the state because I believed God said so. It was lingering at the top of Florida, and I was praying and had a tremendous compassion for Governor Crist, who was dealing with flooding there. It caused me to press in and pray. On this network, twenty hours later, the mocking was tremendous everywhere I went. Twenty-three hours later God did what He said, and it was gone! What if I gave up in the twenty-second hour? My heart of compassion was moved on behalf of the people of the land, and my heart to reveal my Daddy that I know is good was so strong, I could not let go. What God had said when that storm initially started heading to Tampa, where I live, was that it would be like an earlier storm that I took authority over when I took the kids to the beach. We all took forever to get ready and had a long drive to the beach, then we finally got there, paid money to get into the state park, and once we got all our stuff out onto the beach, the darkest, darkest sky started moving quickly toward the beach. All the people started quickly grabbing their chairs and towels and running to their cars. Amid it all, like a crazy person I was praising God, Hallelujah! Aloud. I was loosing the breath of God and rebuking the storm and telling it to go! People were looking at me like I was crazy. It went around us on both sides. And right in the middle on us, the sun came out clearly and shone on us all day. The storm had moved to the north and sat there but did not come near us. A huge rainbow came out and there was a wedding. Thank God I prayed like a crazy woman. The wedding couple was incredibly happy and so were we! When this tropical storm that I was speaking of that had Governor Crist in a crisis started heading toward us, I prayed and God said it would follow the pattern and do the same thing as the thunderstorm at the beach. It went around us and sat on the north of Florida, moving very slowly. The projection was the storm would hover for three days, and it started flooding. That is when God said to give it twenty-four hours. He wanted to make a statement and show that He is God and He is good. He takes us from faith to faith. The Bible says in Revelation 12:11 that we overcome by the blood of the lamb and the word of our testimony. In Romans 10:17, it says faith comes by hearing and hearing by the Word of God. Our faith increases from earlier miracles or seeing miracles in others or reading the Word of God, the Bible, and all the miracles that He performed for them. In Hebrews 13:8, the Word says, "He is the same yesterday, today and forever." We must believe that He is good and He is a rewarder of those that diligently seek Him. A lot of the churches today believe that miracles were only for that time during the Bible. That does not even make sense. God is the same God, with the same character. But He can only move in and through us according to our childlike faith. We are not God, and we are not omnipresent, and it is hard to have compassion in some place where we do not even see or know what is going on. We are not God; we are not omnipresent. Because I have flowed in miracles, I have been persecuted and accused of insanity. I've been asked, if there was ever a storm or destruction elsewhere, why didn't I do something to stop it? That is ridiculous. My hope is that the knowledge of the Glory of the Lord will spread and fill this earth as waters cover the sea. So all people will pray with such a degree of compassion and power for their friends and loved ones, that we will all flow in the miraculous and see God move on our behalf. We must understand God cannot supersede man's will. We must invite Him and let Him in. But I am not God and do not have all power, and some people do not even want to live in the protection of God and reject it. Jesus could do no miracles in some areas because He was not received. And some things we will never have an answer for because we are not God. There is a bad devil. In Revelation 12, we see he hates God's people and seed and spews out floods because he hates us. Ultimately, we overcome by the blood of Jesus, regardless of anything we go through and things we don't know or have answers for. This is called our cross, where we are taught in Romans 8:18 that the weight of suffering we may go through regardless of our faith, our faith holds on to the promise of God's goodness, knowing the weight of suffering is not even to be compared to the weight of Glory that is about to be revealed in and through us as we believe.

Joseph had a dream when he was a young boy, and thirty years later it manifested. He never saw the pain and the torment of being betrayed by those he loved or falsely accused in his dream. That is called the cross. We hold on to the dream, the Word, the hope of the goodness of God in the land of the living, even when circumstances are contrary or it seems to be taking longer than we think it should. The Bible says in 2 Peter 3:8 that a day is as a thousand years and a thousand years as a day. God is not bound by an earthly time. When He speaks or even thinks something, it is done in the spirit realm before it manifests in the natural. As someone that is used to getting immediate miracle results in some areas, I have other areas when the pain is so great and the cross is so heavy, I understand like He said in Romans 8:18, the weight of that kind of suffering is not to even be compared to the glory that is about to be revealed in us. If we hold on, He will show up and show off so big and gloriously, all we will see is that He is for Us, He loves us, He will never ever forsake us. So, hold on, do not let go of Him. And that is a place of surrender. The truth is, this world is so temporal, it will not last. But the kingdom of God is forever, and since I work and live in the kingdom of God, miracles will happen in my life on this earth. Once my purpose is done, I can go live forever where there are no tears, there are no fights of faith to overcome evil. I will reign forever with my King Daddy. It is my compassion and heart that everyone here goes with me and faces him one day and hears, "Well done, thy good and faithful servant." The thought of even one person on this earth not making it to heaven but living for eternity with the devil that torments innocent people and robs, kills, and destroys is more than my heart can handle. If the difference is from me and you doing all we can do and surrender to His power to let Him be God to save the lost, how could we ever do anything else? I think heaven can wait in my mind, I can go there when I am done. For now I must reveal the one and only true God in this earth. And that means to take Him at His Word! I assure you and most solemnly say to you, anyone who believes in Me as savior will also do the things that I do, and he will do even greater things than these in extent and outreach, because I am going to the Father (John 14:12). He said to them, "Why are you afraid, you men of little faith?" then He got up and rebuked the winds and the sea, and there was at once a great and wonderful calm, a perfect peacefulness. The men wondered in amazement saying, "What kind of man is this, that even the winds and the sea obey him? (Matt. 8:26–27) The steadfast love of the Lord never ceases, his mercies never come to an end: they are new every morning: great is your faithfulness (Lam. 3:22–23). Now faith is the assurance, the title deed, the confirmation of things hoped for and divinely guaranteed, and the evidence of things not seen, the conviction of their reality, faith comprehends as fact what cannot be experienced by the physical senses (Heb. 11:1). Again I say to you, that if two believers on earth agree, that is, are of one mind, in harmony, about anything that they ask within the will of God, it will be done for them by My Father in heaven (Matt. 18:19). But without faith it is impossible to walk with God and please Him, for whoever comes near to God must necessarily believe that God exists and that He rewards those who earnestly and diligently seek him (Heb. 11:6).

Chapter 11

WE MUST BE IN LOVE WITH JESUS AS OUR BRIDEGROOM

All through the scriptures, we see that Jesus is our bridegroom, and we as the body of Christ are His bride. He is coming back for his bride, and we will celebrate at the great wedding feast in heaven for all of eternity. He is coming for a bride without spot or wrinkle. Speaking of our garments, as we study garments in the Word, in Colossians 3:14, we see we are told to put on love like a garment, and in Isaiah 61:3, we are told to put on a spirit of praise instead of a spirit of heaviness. This is the bride He is coming for, clothed in love and adoration for her King. The Word tells us in Matthew 25:4 to keep our lamps burning brightly and full of oil and not be asleep, but to be alert and watching and expecting him to come for us. Like a lover waiting for her love to finally take her away to their dream home. Song of Solomon is a whole chapter in the Bible of a beautiful love story between King Solomon and his beautiful bride-to-be and the love story leading to the wedding day and consummation of their union physically. All throughout the chapter, we see this is an illustration of our great love with our bridegroom, Jesus. The truth is that we are not only a bride awaiting our bridegroom, but we must be in love. How can we not be in love with him? As we read the scriptures of Matthew, Mark, Luke, and John, we see his beautiful character. A man that left all of heaven to take on flesh and blood and become one of us, to win our hearts and woo us to follow him and love him forever. As we study his character, we find a man that gave his very life for us. He did not just come preaching and teaching and demonstrating power, he took it to the utmost level of love anyone could have, and that was to lay down his life for us so we could live. Everything we go through on this earth that hurts, he confronted and took on the devil himself, sin, and death and overcame for us. He was a man with the sperm of God, God, and man in the flesh. Part of him wanted to say forget this, this is too hard. We see in the garden before his death in Luke 22:44, he prayed with such intensity that he sweat great drops of blood, asking God if he could produce a different plan. Asking the Father if He could please take this cup from him. But He surrendered and said not my will, but your will be done. He took on every disease, sickness, poverty, sin, and overcame so He could bury them finally and arise in resurrection power. He did this so we would not have to live in eternal damnation because of sin, but so that we could live an abundant, healthy life on this earth that transcends into eternity in love with our savior.

Once again, I remind you, we must be in love with Him! In Revelation 2, the Holy Spirit is speaking to one of the churches, saying, "I see everything you have done, and that you are doing for the good. Your works are good, but I have something against you, you forgot your first love, Jesus." The truth is that we must be in love with this wonderful man, Jesus. We will then see the direct result of power in our lives. It is the direct result of joy that gives us strength to endure whatever we face on this earth, knowing we will see this beautiful savior that loved us so much he had to do something to reach us, to teach us and keep us forever. Why are we so in love with him? Because he is so in love with us! Talk about jumping through hoops and over walls to get to us. At the announcement of his birth, there was an edict sent out by King Herod to kill all the first-born babies. The devil knew the prophecy of the Messiah. Jesus lived and overcame even as a tiny baby because hell cannot stop the perfect love of God. As he grew and it was evident to all that knew him that he was the son of God, he couldn't help but go, even as a young boy, to study and set himself apart in knowledge and power, as he spent time with the Father to fulfill the very reason he left the streets of gold in heaven and came covered in flesh to save us. As He became an adult, he endured grievous opposition from those that were so afraid there would be a takeover because he had such a large following. The pride and foolishness of man raging in a jealous war of humanity against divinity. The flesh is enmity against the living Word of God Himself. He faced it head on and overcame, even for those that crucified Him. And He prayed, "Father, forgive them, they do not even know what they are doing." This is true love; what man loves enemies and tries to rescue them from their sin and eternal damnation? Jesus, that man showed the love of God and overcame the pride and flesh of humanity for even his haters with blood-bought love for all that would receive. This gift of eternal life and forgiveness of sins extended even to his enemies and those that were jealous of Him. He was in no competition with them and their kingdom, and was after their hearts, presenting the kingdom of God. Why did he have such a large following? Because everywhere he went, he took on the fight of every man, woman, and child he met. He fought their sickness if they were sick and healed all. If they were lacking, he came and spoke with such love and care, and caused a great overflow of abundance that overcame their lack. He stared death down and overcame, and pulled his friends out of their graves. He is life and life eternal. We will never die or fear death spiritually because of this man, Jesus. We are alive forever to rule and reign with him because of what he did for us. It is the perfect knight in shining armor story. The most amazing thing about this story is that it is the truth, it is not fictional! Taste and see that he is good! In John 2:1–11, Jesus was at a wedding feast of his friends, and the wine ran out before the party was over.

His mother beckoned him to bring a solution to the problem. Not only is He concerned with saving us from hell, he wants to give us an enjoyable time and good days on this earth. He told her to fill water pots with water and then He spoke the living Word and turned the water into wine. He is a giver, lacking nothing, because he is supernatural. Anyone who receives this gift of eternal life receives His same spirit and love and lives in us and becomes one with us, as our gloriously bridegroom. Truth be told, why do so many people listen to me? Not because I am so talented or good looking. Truth be told, why am I able to flow with so many signs, wonders, and miracles in this earth? I am in love with this glorious man, Jesus, and I want nothing but Him in my life and on this earth!

Chapter 12
A Quest for Truth Can Only Be Found and Answered in the Bible

One Thing I have found is truth is not based on different theologies or man's opinion. It is not based on what our parents have always believed or pastors have told us. We see in Mark 7:8 that it is the traditions of men that hold back the power of God in our lives. That must mean the Holy Spirit, who is called the Spirit of Truth, can be hindered by traditions or beliefs that have been passed down through generations and generations. Many churches preach that God may heal some people; otherwise, it may be a thorn in your flesh you must suffer, and then it really becomes a matter of faith that is not steadfast because God may or may not do it, depending on whether he feels like it or not. Any thorn in our flesh that does not go away even after we pray again and again will eventually be conquered by all sufficient grace. It is not a question of faith but a work of God's enabling grace that transcends into a realm of faith and favor that we never could have gotten. To really hold on by faith, we must know that his grace is all sufficient. And when we feel like we cannot hold on any longer, in our very weakness is when his power and his grace is made strong. It is in our very weakness of realizing we cannot do this, but he can do this. It is called all sufficient grace; it is a total surrender to his power and strength. When I went on a quest for truth on healing, I studied Jesus, since he is the direct representation of God on the earth.

He said if you have seen me, you have seen the father. Jesus only healed and never came to a gravesite except to raise the dead. When it comes to storms, people look at the scenario of the disciples in the boat in a storm or Peter walking on water in the storm, but to Jesus there was no storm. Even if there was one, He walked on water and it did not bother him whatsoever. He spoke and the wind and waves obeyed him. We take this challenge to search for the truth of a matter in our spirit, because why live unless we are living in truth? Who wants to get through life and find out they lived a lie because they did not search for truth? The Bible says that the glory of a king is to search out a matter. The world is in chaos and strife and discouraged, even suicidal because they are in a debate of truth or deception. Someone is right and someone is wrong. Everyone cannot be right if they have a difference of opinion on a matter. Some people believe that is truth, that we can agree to disagree, and it really does not matter. But how can you let people go to hell that have believed a lie, or let them die in sickness and disease if God has made a way to live? Or live in destruction when Jesus came to this earth to give us life and life more abundantly and gave us the same power in our mouths that he had in his mouth? All these things surround darkness, and gross darkness will fill this earth as we get closer to the Lord's return, but he also said these days would be as in the days of Noah. We will have the ark of deliverance. We have the anointing as God's people to be saved and not even a hair on our head will be harmed if he finds faith when he comes with the answer, the solution, the deliverance that we need.

As you search for truth, you may find you feel alone quite often because the majority will not take the risk and step out in truth because we live in a world of deception. The flesh wants to fit in. The government may take you captive or kill you if you disagree with them, but hold fast only to what the Word of God has to say concerning a matter. The world will mock you. I would rather stand before God at His bema seat in truth and hear, "Well done, thy good and faithful servant," than to fit in with the crowd here on earth. You may feel alone at times because not everyone will receive you. They would rather blame God or say, "Faith doesn't work." The truth is we are not alone, and as we walk in truth and follow Christ, we will find that we have a following who are on a quest for truth and will follow the ways of God as well. We are not alone, although as a trailblazer and revolutionist, you will feel alone since you started a movement of truth against a flow of deception. When you start blazing your trail of truth and enlightenment to a lost and dying world, you will hear, "Faith does not work. Prayer didn't work for me." We still spark up faith and shine the light of God's Word! Faith is unseen. It does not let go until it breaks through into truth and what you are believing for finally manifests. Our confession of truth or faith does not change; the circumstances will start changing if you hold onto truth tenaciously and never let go!

Chapter 13

THE HOLY SPIRIT IS TRUTH

The Bible says that the Holy Spirit is called the Spirit of Truth. It is through Him that we can know truth. This spirit of truth is meant to lead us and guide us in every area of life. He is called a paraklete, comforter, meant to always be with us. He is also called the Helper. Being filled with the Holy Spirit will lead us into all truth. As we empty ourselves of self and fill up with Him and submit ourselves to His leading, we will always find ourselves in the truth of a matter. He is omniscient, so He knows all things. As we pray and submit to the Holy Spirit, we will begin to manifest the gifts of the spirit. We can also work in what is called a word of knowledge. That is when we know something by the spirit and would have no way of knowing except through the gift of the Holy Spirit. That is why He is called a witness. We pray and He gives a witness of the Holy Spirit, in a word of prophecy, a dream, or a strong gut feeling that you cannot explain otherwise, except it is Him and it is truth. He is one with the Living Word. The way the Holy Spirit will work in our lives is by revealing the Word. A preacher could be preaching, but under the anointing of the Holy Spirit there is understanding of the Word. I cannot live without the Word! The Holy Spirit has revealed through the Word my right to be healed, so I manifest healing in my body and soul. I am anointed to heal others in the name of Jesus. By studying Jesus, the living Word, and the miracles of Jesus in the Word, I have become not just a hearer but a doer of the Word, understanding that He gave us the

Holy Spirit. We see in John 14:12 where Jesus said that we would do the works that He did and even greater. In areas of destruction and natural disasters—storms, terror, drought and earthquakes—the Holy Spirit has revealed to me through the life of Jesus our redemptive right to speak the Word of God to anything that comes to rob, kill, and destroy our lives. And that as I speak it, we see in Isaiah 55:11 that the Word will never return void because it is sent by the power of the Holy Spirit, and God is true to watch over His own Word. And that the same power that was in Jesus's mouth is the same Word of God that is in our mouth as we speak in faith! The Holy Spirit has revealed the Word in manifesting the fruit of the spirit, so I am without excuse as a child of God to shine as His child and love and treat others as Jesus would treat them and care for them. Because it is not of myself but the living Word at work in and through me. The Holy Spirit has revealed to me and helped me understand the Word by speaking in tongues, so I do not just read it, but the Word has its lead place in my life for the perfect will of God beyond my finite human understanding. The Holy Spirit brings the Word to my remembrance so when I need it pertaining to anything in life, my mind has become the mind of Christ, by the renewing of my mind in the Word by the help of the Holy Spirit. The Holy Spirit has helped me understand the Word in our full redemption from the curse of the law, so I will not settle for anything except the manifestation of the Word, no matter how long it seems to take. The Holy Spirit helps me do this by the fruit of the spirit called patience. Patience gives me the tenacity to hold on by faith, faith fueled by the living Word. The Holy Spirit's fruit is love, so I understand how the Word works because I have the love of God that fuels faith in area of life! It has been the planting of the Word by the watering of the living Holy Spirit, living waters that the Word has sprung forth into every situation needed pertaining to this life and to be a Godly woman. I cannot live without the Word that is one with the Holy Spirit for even a second in any area of life! The Living Word is always working, even when we do not understand or see what God is doing in the natural. When I first moved to California, there was a four-year drought and wildfires started by demonic madmen that went on for twelve months out of the year. Neighborhoods were going up in smoke, and fear gripped the state and people around the nation. A couple of years before I moved to California, I had a dream that I had moved to California and was laying down my life in a church. The church was in a storefront. I am not sure what the storefront means, but I had butterflies on my face. There was more to the dream. I had a long technology train behind me with people from other nations on it and it was dark, as in evil. My mom was standing outside of the train, meaning she was standing with me in agreement against the darkness and evil. But there was a famous democrat on the train that had a very full plate, and he was falling asleep. I was trying to reach for him to pray for him since the full plate meant he was overwhelmed, and the sleeping meant he really did not know what was going on with the darkness of those surrounding him and needed an awakening. Everyone around me was trying to keep me from reaching him to pray, but he started reaching to me and wanted prayer. I could not figure out what the butterflies were.

Once I moved to the brown, dry land scorched by wildfires, I started praying for rain. God kept saying it is coming and it looks a cloud the size of a man's hand. That went on for about a year once I started praying. I asked God what He meant since it is what Elijah's servant said before the rains came that Elijah prayed for. He told me it was an awakening to the prophetic. The fivefold ministry is like a man's hand. The pastor, the prophet, the evangelist, the teacher, and the apostle. All have been received in most religious circles and society, except the prophet. Many times, the prophet confronts corruption and, like the prophet Elijah, does wonderous miracles for the awakening to the ways and heart and power of

God. Prophets send out a clarion call for repentance. They do not dress in religious garb and do not spend time in religious circles. In fact, the Bible tells us that God picks the weak and foolish to confound the wise, the ones that do not seem to fit in but are driven with a passion and love for God to save the lost and prepare the world for His return, while revealing his character to a sleeping world. One night after about a year of living in California, I put on a video of rain. When I woke in the night, I heard the sound of rain in my spirit and all morning in prayer, and it started raining that day and continued. It rained so much that California experienced what is called a super bloom. As I was driving on the highway and through residential neighborhoods everywhere, there were masses of butterflies. It was all over the news and newspapers. People were in awe of the butterflies that came to California because of the super bloom. Driving around, it was the most beautiful thing we had ever seen, and people were stopping everywhere to take pictures of the flowers amid the green, clean landscaping. God blessed the land with rain and the wildfires stopped. This is an example of the leading of the spirit of truth. Even when we do not understand what God is doing, He is always sure to reveal Himself. I am in constant awe of him. I honesty cannot remember all the miracles he has worked in and through me by faith. After I had been in California for about a year, there was a category 5 hurricane heading for Tampa, where my friends and family were. I prayed for about three nights and woke to pray, and still it kept heading there with a vengeance. The Lord gave me a word that I posted on Facebook that the waves would be under our feet. By the time the storm reached Tampa, it dissipated to a tropical storm, but even so the surge and waves would cause dangerous flooding. That afternoon, everyone was posting news videos and private videos of the whole area, the beaches and bays, because of the dry ground. The Holy Spirit that is one with Jesus, the living Word, was prophetically sent and overcame the tumult of the waves and surge. The waters disappeared like the parting of the Red Sea. Meteorologists were afraid it would be a tsunami. It seemed like something out of a movie. I said, "No, it is a miracle. The wind of God held back the surge and waves." It was beautiful. It was exactly that because the water came slowly back into place. God preformed this same miracle when I moved back to Florida and Hurricane Ian was heading straight twards us. I live on a small island surrounded by a bay connected to the ocean. As the storm was approaching I saw Jesus walking on the water the night before in a vision and he literally did just that and preformed the same miracle and caused the whole bay and ocean to disappear so instead of swimming with sharks I was watching Jesus show up again like the Savior that He is! Another amazing example of the living Word is the power of the name of Jesus spoken prophetically. When I first came to California, as I was driving all around for hours and hours doing my job, selling solar, I would see in the spirit realm destruction everywhere. I would hear the prophets calling for destruction in the land since so many had blatantly rejected the Lord, and I was crying mercy over the land. I opened right up in the Word, and God said where the Angel was calling for destruction, another called to seal the heads for salvation, to give an opportunity to repent and come to know the goodness of God. My girls and I were sitting in our living room when an earthquake hit California, a little over 7.0 on the Richter scale, the worst in strength for many years. The last earthquake that had been that strong wiped out miles of Long Beach and caused destruction. This time when it happened, one of my daughters was sitting on the couch with me, and it seemed like the coffee table moved slightly, but we could not be sure. The second I felt movement, I said, "Jesus!" In the one second it took to say His name, the shaking stopped in our house. I said to my daughter, "Did you move the table for a second?" and she said, "No, I wondered if you did." Then we noticed my other daughter on FaceTime with her friend in Chino, an hour away, and her friend's house was shaking for a whole minute. We found out that all of California shook for a whole minute, eight hours north of Los Angeles all the way south of us to San Diego. But in my house, it was only for a second while I said the name of Jesus! I am constantly in awe. Even my neighbors said their house shook for a whole minute. The amazing miracle is God saved the land, and there was not one injury or destroyed building whatsoever. Proverbs 18:10 says the name of the Lord is a strong tower, the righteous run in and are saved. I have found this to be the absolute truth!

Chapter 14

You Must Learn to Survive to Thrive and Then Revive

Have you ever been in a race and at that last round when your legs feel like rubber? You are seconds from the finish line with what seems like no breath in your lungs. You may have even overcome some people trying to trip you or boo you along that last round, but you know that you are the champion. You just need to take that last soar through the air to get your leg over that finish line!

Have you ever been in childbirth and pushing for thirty minutes in pain, waiting for the head to crown? You look at the mirror they place at the breakthrough point, so you can stay focused in that moment of intense pressure and pain. You want it to finally be over, but it is still going on, and the labor pains keep coming. It seems to be taking too long, yet you have no choice but to keep pushing, focusing, breathing, and envisioning the life you are travailing for, knowing that soon you will have the beautiful reason resting on your bosom for all the pain you are experiencing. You know you must finish.

What about living in a world where nothing makes sense? Living in a world that you know should be a land of justice and freedom and liberty for all, and where you know there is evil and the kingdom of darkness is against the kingdom of light. Yet it seems like the kingdom of darkness is getting away with murder, injustice, and deception. Again and again,

God has proven for all to see that you are in His kingdom of light! He gave you a voice to speak the truth and reveal the heart of God and lead people in the ways of God, so much so that he answered prayers again and again and backed His word with signs, wonders, and miracles for all to see. Miracles that stood against destruction and terror, and brought healing and supernatural intervention of God's goodness. He had to do such wonders, signs, and miracles because the snake, the devil himself, was in pursuit of you because you had led so many to the one and only true God of love and spirit and truth. You exposed the devil's deception, and he hated you and was jealous that you had such a following that had come to know the Lord.

Yet, the pursuit of the snake was still being allowed in the land for all to see. Just like they saw the wonders of God's goodness, they saw injustice, mistreatment, and bullying of the innocent. It is still going on, and you must wake up, lead, pray, and have mercy on those that have done you wrong. You must pray and love them even though there seems to be no difference or change in your life's situation. You think, amid injustice and pain, that surely justice will prevail in the land. God has already shown justice in your life, so what could be against you? Then you realize you have a responsibility to God to intercede and pray for the land because He is jealous for His land and His own creation that He made to have a relationship with Himself. And you realize He is the one that you are fighting for, He is the one you must prevail, travail, and overcome for. He wants their souls, and because you love Him, you love His creation, even those that have seriously done you wrong and been unjust. Jesus took on the form of flesh and blood and came to the world because our Father in heaven loved the world so much that He had a plan to save the world. Jesus came and the very ones that He came to save mocked him, bullied him, mistreated him, and killed him in complete and utter injustice. They put him on the cross that was made for a criminal when He had not deserved it. He cried out to God and asked Him to have mercy and forgive them, because they didn't even know what they were doing. He knew if they had known, they wouldn't be doing it. We are told to take up our crosses and follow Him. We realize we are in the last days, and that means pre-tribulation, tribulation of the church. That means persecution, that means there is a real devil, just like there is a real God and savior. And if we are in the kingdom of God's love and light, that devil hates us. But greater is He that is in us than He that is in the world. Rev. 5:5 says to fear not, weep not, during these days. We have read the story, we know He is the author and the finisher, and we must finish! He already has won, He already has conquered that devil, sin, and death and given us the keys to the kingdom! We must wake up, we must breathe, we must focus, we must push, we must travail, we must prevail, we must run the race set before us, because we have a more sure word of prophecy that we will overcome because of this wonderful savior, the Messiah, Jesus Christ. His blood was enough, His redemption was enough. He always finishes what he starts! He is the beginning, and He is the end. He already showed us the victory, and we win! I should say won, because what we must realize is a prophecy is already complete. Like the turning of an hourglass, a day is as a thousand years in the kingdom of God and a thousand years as a day. A kyros is a God moment. He already won for us, in our God moment, and the more sure word of prophecy is manifesting on this earth. Understanding and knowing this is what gives us a strong assurance so that we can rest in our spirit man and in His truth and not fear or weep or despair. It gives us joy in our hope of glory in Christ; it strengthens us, even when we are still questioning: When will this injustice, deception, and darkness that we are up against end? This is how I survive, thrive, and revive, knowing the plan and victory for my life's story is already complete and alive and about to break through, crossing over and overcoming every opposition, as God promised and showed me. God's character is to never withhold good from us; it is to overflow us with His goodness and provision. The devil hates us and wants to steal the glory of God. He wants to pound us down, take our stuff, and take our dignity. He is jealous of us and that is why his job, the Bible says, is to try to wear down God's people. So, if you sense there is someone working to try to destroy you and break you down, you are up against the devil. It is never God, and it is never the character of God. You must know what is true. If you believe a lie and give the enemy control over your life, you will believe God is doing something to you. Of course, we would never think God is doing something, but when some type of wrong or injustice goes on for a long time, God's people may question why God is allowing it. He has shown up and shown Himself to be with us, to be strong amid impossible situations. To supernaturally answer prayers to the point that the world saw God intervene on our behalf. So how could this still be going on, how could he be allowing this? The answer is that he is giving those that have done us wrong a chance to repent. It is not His will that any perish. Jesus even said before He came that the world was not convicted of sin. As we are filled with the spirit of God, the spirit of truth, and His great love, we are patient in long suffering, full of compassion and loving kindness. God's anger only lasts a moment, the Bible says. As we are filled and consumed with the spirit of God, we realize there is purpose to our pain. The purpose is souls. Our lives bring conviction to the wrong so mankind can repent and get in alignment and ready for the return of the Lord. As Christians, we may get so wrapped up in our lives, families, and being blessed that we forget the one main reason we are here—for the great commission. The great commission is why we are alive, why we survive, why we thrive, and why we revive and revive others. We have the good news. We are filled with Jesus. As we fellowship in his sufferings, we also fellowship in his resurrection power. When we leave this earth and get to heaven, we will bring nothing except souls.

The Bible says that before the Lord's return and before the day of the Lord, regardless of what injustice and wrong evil men got away with, God's justice will come and finally vindicate His own and judge the world, those that rejected His spirit and truth. But before that day comes, Jesus said the spirit of Elijah must come. If you study Elijah's life, you will see that God used him to confront injustice in the land. When He spoke for the rain to come and prophesied, "I hear the sound of the abundance of rain," it rained. He performed such signs, wonders, and miracles to waken the people of the day and the false prophets to the one and only true living God, that He was God and God alone. The spirit of Elijah is the spirit of Abba. It will turn the hearts of the fathers to the children and the children to the true Fathers, the good Fathers. It will turn earthly fathers to the heart of God, so they become spiritual fathers and operate in the heart of the Father God with a heavenly mindset. It will turn the unscrupulous back to the wisdom of the upright. God's goodness and open show of power and spirit will lead man to repentance. Romans 8 tells us we have not been given this world's spirit, a spirit of fear, but a spirit of Abba, which is a spirit of adoption, a spirit of Elijah. I believe the spirit of Elijah has come.

So, if you have the purpose and assignment on earth to pray and teach God's heart to the unscrupulous, know you are filled with the love of God or He would not choose you for such a task. Jesus said, "What is love if you just love those that love you and treat you right? No, the true show of love is to love even your enemies or those that mistreat you." You are there to save their soul and reveal God's heart and goodness and unconditional love, so they can repent and become children of God. It is that love working on the inside that will cause you to endure injustice or wrong that has been done to you. In the Bible, Joseph was thrown into a pit. He was under—financially and emotionally—and his soul was tempted to be discouraged by their actions. To be sold like a commodity and a slave.

To feel stuck in a situation they created without good cause. It was wrong, but God had a greater cause and Joseph, by the spirit of God, knew this. He said what they did was wrong, but God has used it for the good to save many souls alive. Therefore, we endure, survive, to then thrive and revive and encourage others in these days.

DEVOTIONALS

I have included thirty devotionals, so you can read one a day. I pray they will minister to your heart! Remember to meditate on what God says, and He will keep your heart and mind in Christ Jesus.

"My Love, My Sons, and Daughters...I have never failed you! The enemy of your soul and life is NOT greater than my great love and power for you! REMEMBER, meditate, ponder how AGAIN and AGAIN and AGAIN and AGAIN and AGAIN and AGAIN and AGAIN and AGAIN and AGAIN and AGAIN and AGAIN and AGAIN I broke through at the sound of your heart cry! That is why the enemy hates you and tries to lord over you. The earth belongs to Me, I see all, I know all, I know the schematics of the enemy against you because of your heart and trust in Me. I also know your heart that has taken on my heart, that believes My love and power is greater and has literally come to save the world from deception, injustice, and a spirit of slavery! Fear Not, my thoughts are HIGHER, REMAIN in my heartbeat, KEEP My mind amid persecution, and your reward and Joy will be great, My kingdom is Yours!" Abba

"What you thought was the end, when you think you have had all you can take from the haters, the snake, the enemy of your soul...you must know it is only the beginning of what I am about to do to turn your whole life around, My Love! Never compare yourself among yourselves, that is where you lose yourself! You are my unique representation of a part of my heart that I want to reveal to the world! I am always doing a new thing, a new thing in you, a new thing in the earth, a new thing no one has thought of except the Creator of Heaven and Earth, creating in and through you, My Love! I made you to rise above the norm, above the storm! Lift up your Head, your Redemption draweth Nigh, say only Recompense is Mine!" Your Living Redeemer

"Keep your Eyes on Me, My Love. Look at nothing else, listen to nothing else except Me! I have called you; I have chosen you. Know that some will receive you and some will not. You didn't choose me; I chose you and I am well pleased with you! Say what I say, having done all, stand as my grace empowers you to endure. You will not lose your crown as you remain in me and I in you! Strength comes as you see what I see, and that My love is what I have already won for you, victory, healing, and restoration for you and your whole family and nation!" Your Prince of Peace, Jesus Christ!

"As a mother hen gathers her chicks, I am bringing about a gathering, a refuge of refreshing, strengthening restoration to my people! A shelter of healing where peace is imparted, curses are broken off many generations, and a rebirth and regeneration of my ways are established from the least to the greatest! All belong. I am calling the so-called ugly, the so-called beautiful, the weak, the strong! I am calling the least to the greatest, the poor and the rich in the estimation of men, women, and every child to be sealed by my grace and kept and held steadfast by my great love and care! They will live and breathe and move in the confidence of being called Sons and Daughters of God!" Your El Shaddai

"Everything I put in your heart, the seed of my word took root and is coming forth speedily, my kingdom is springing forth all the way to the finish line of your faith! Keep watering it with your tears of thanksgiving, knowing what was spoken deep in your heart cannot be uprooted because it is so embedded in my love and heart for you, my child! I placed the desires of my heart in your heart and the moment you said be it unto me according to your word, it took root!

Watch my love, watch my power, watch my goodness, watch my deliverance, watch my wisdom, watch my true riches, watch the nations, watch that covenant relationship, watch my church, watch your children, watch your children's children grow and come forth into complete fruition, my love! You will see with your natural eyes what your spirit eye saw a long time ago! Take courage, it's the same power that rose Jesus from that dead, springing forth in your every desire, fulling My desire and kingdom come on the earth as it is in Heaven!" Abba

"Listen to my spirit deep in your heart, walk by faith and not by sight! Faith is rising within you. Awaken purpose, stir up the gift on the inside, and take the kingdom by force! Take dominion of your land, take dominion over fear, lack, injustice, and hold on! I am not as far off as you would suppose due to circumstances. I am doing a deep work, a work I started and will be faithful to complete in you, my Love! The end result at hand, within your reach, is Perfect Love!" Your Faithful King of all Kings, Jehovah Jirah, Shalom, Nissi, Rapha

"I formed you intricately and called you and chose you as my masterpiece creation. I knew you then and I know you now! The enemy of your life wanted to take your life and still does, but my angels have placed a hedge of protection around you and my resurrection power is greater! I took the keys of hell and death and am breathing life into your body, soul, and land! Fear not, dwell in me and I will dwell in you, set your affections on my desires, I own it all, the earth and all that I created belongs to me! As I move through your hands, feet, and mouth, we take back every child, gift, and nation out of deception and bring them into my marvelous light! Hold on and don't let go of Me! I will finish what I started in and through you, my child!" Says the Lord of Host

"My Beloved, I left the 99 in search of just you! When you were in pain, I carried you close to my heart. There, you listened, you trusted, you hoped, you believed, you received all my power, my sight and might! Now I call

you to lead the way, My way, the Highway, the Love way, the Right way! Take it High, take My praise High, take my Glory High, take My Name High! Now look....
They are following Us, they are loving, obeying, and showing My finished work at the cross was not in vain! Well done, My love, this is my Glory, the Father glorified in Me, He and I in and through you, My Child of the Living God!" The Eternal Living Lamb of God

"You have chosen the good part, My Love, sitting at my feet. There is nothing I love more than when you listen to my heart, wait expectantly for my voice, and rest in the peace I won for you amid the world you are living in! I did it all for you so you could have it all, I paid the full price of your redemption. There is nothing lacking or missing. I have lifted and carried you when you thought you couldn't take another step, my feet have walked in your shoes as I confronted and overcame every demonic spirit in hell, as I walked about doing good to all that would receive Me! When I beckoned you to follow in my footsteps, you followed and you have walked as One with Me, and this is just the beginning! Hold on, think of Me, I am coming soon, we have all of eternity to share the depths of My Love, the Wonder and the Mysteries of My ever-revealing heart and goodness!" Jesus

"PEACE I give to you, not as this world gives, do I give to you. Let not your heart be troubled. Trust in Me. In this world you will have trouble, but TAKE COURAGE in the depths of your heart, hold on to my heart, I have already overcome the world!" Jesus

"The Birds are not worried, my Love; I know when each one needs to eat and exactly what they need when they need my loving care. I have created you as the center-piece of my joy. You are of more value than all the birds from the farthest nations in the east to the expanse of the west! My Father's heart is made full in your trust in my goodness, care, and provision in every need you have. I love that you look to Me first and make every move and go about your days looking to Me to lead and for all that you need and desire! The earth belongs to Me, My love, I own it, I lack nothing, and I made it for you to enjoy! You are never alone, I have never left you for a minute, I see all that goes on and your mistreatment and how you have loved despite of it and looked to Me. Now get ready to see How I have noticed!" Abba

"Because of the finished work of My Son, I have remembered MY Covenant Promises to you and I am pouring out the treasures of my Heart more than you feel you can handle! I am increasing your capacity and enlarging you so that YOU will even be amazed at what pours out of you! Your mouth, your heart, your bank account, your gifts, your children's and grandchildren's gifts, your church, your whole family, your nation will increase and overflow with an outpouring of kingdom prosperity and peace! My standard of good is greater than this earth has yet to see, my end revival and restoration as in Joel 2 will be beyond any of my earlier outpourings!

Look UP, Look at Me, Hear Me, My Child, it's already started!!" Your Redeemer, El Shaddai

"As you pray for willing hearts, my Love, I am breaking up the fallow ground of their hearts! Softening the hardness caused by the things of this world in those you love and care for, and even your enemies! I will keep your heart tender as you continue to pray for those that do you wrong intentionally or unintentionally, the blessing will come on you and those you pray for in such a measure it will blow your mind! You are coming into such a place of peace, regardless of circumstances, because you have chosen the good part of a peacemaker following your Prince of Peace! I am with you, I will never leave you or forsake you unto the ends of the earth. Take up your cross and follow Me into everlasting peace powered by My great love!" Father, Son, Holy Spirit—With you, for you, in you, all around you.

God is saying, "Remember every time I came through for you, every answer to every prayer you ever prayed! I have never failed you, in every place you added another rock, another revealed manifestation of your redemption as you built an altar of thanksgiving, my love! Every rock of remembrance of the revealing of my Son in all His goodness and resurrection power was built in your life that you now abide and dwell in! Remaining in the Name above every Name is your fortress, your refuge, the joy of your strength! Again and again you have praised Me, full of thanksgiving at that altar before you have seen the manifestation of my answers in your current situations! I am greatly pleased with you, My Love. Hold on, I heard you the first time you prayed, there has been a warfare for your destiny, you will prevail and overcome, and the gates of hell will not prevail against you!"

"My eye is on the Sparrow, everything that concerns you concerns Me. My resurrection power and love are greater than death and hell! I only have good plans for you. Plans for your future, full of hope that manifests into a living substance of faith generated by love to fulfill every vision, dream, and desire I put in you! I see great prosperity for you and your loved ones. I am married to you and your Land!" Your Ishi

"Fear not, weep not! I AM always with you, be still and know that I am God! I have called you as my unique representative of my power and goodness on this earth, I have made you for signs, wonders, and miracles on the earth! Never forget your purpose! My Resurrection power always comes after you lay down your life in surrender to my call, those that lose their lower life will find their higher life of purpose in Me! Take up your cross and follow me, Rise up in my manifested power, I have given you the keys to the kingdom, now overcome My Love! I AM the Lion of the Tribe of Judah!"

"You are on my mind, my thoughts for you outnumber the sand on the seashore. My love for you is higher than the expanse of heaven reaching all the way back and into eternity! My care for you and willingness to take care of you, my love, is beyond the human comprehension, for I didn't just make a way to provide you with a warm bed, food, drink, but I make a way so your spirit and soul can live on and on and on and on, forever and ever into my highest heaven, my highest glory, my forever care and unfailing unconditional love and care! Do not look at men and think of me, do not compare Me with the misrepresentation of my love and care, I am not a man that I would lie or misuse you and your love and time. Rest in my Heart, because I am at rest in yours!" Abba

"Even as I told Abraham, I am multiplying you as far as the eye can see so shall your descendants be. Those that come to know me through your travail, as you loose my word and kingdom on the earth will multiply and arise and shine with my Glory! As my word is loosed on earth, it is loosed in Heaven! Don't only look, but see, see as far as your natural and spiritual eyes can see. Your influence, your care and heart will multiply through this earth as far as the eye can see, My love! For you have taken on my heart, love, and care, and with me there is no end to My goodness through my Living Word! I am your Great Reward!" Elohim

"There is a river that makes my city glad! Do you not perceive that I AM doing a new thing?! Rivers amid your battle and pain you will see! I AM the Alpha and Omega, the Beginning and the End, every vision, every dream, every desire I placed in you is springing up and coming alive in your space and time! I am well ABLE, and I AM alive forevermore!! I AM the WAY, the TRUTH, and the LIFE, and your very present help in times of trouble! I am making all things New in and through you! Arise and shine, my love. I am showing myself strong on your behalf!" Your Living Redeemer

"My Love, tune in only to My Voice and see what I AM saying! Speak what I see and see what you heard Me say! I AM the Master Creator, and I have made you to create! Remove the old, the pain of yesterday, so your heart does not callous. I am renewing your inner man where my word is growing and flourishing in the tenderness of your heart. LET NOT your heart be troubled, DON'T LET it be afraid! Trust in Me and I will finish the masterpiece of your life, it is beautiful and more than you could ever imagine! Let go and let My life flow throughout your soul, your mouth, your fingers, and write, speak, sing, praise, rejoice, dance, live, breathe, move in Me!
Create, I tell you it is not too late! I have just begun to reveal my heart to this generation, darkness and gross darkness has filled the earth in the hour. Now my church will Arise and Shine in the Glory of the Lord!!" YOUR ABBA

"Your deep is calling out to my deep, and My deep is calling to your deep, my Love! The longing, the pain, the desire for more of Me, more of my Love, more of My heart, and power on the earth and those around you, is My heart longing to release more of my Heart, love, and power in and through you and the earth! Hold nothing back, go deep, find me, I love to be found in all My goodness and glory! My deep desire is for those that do not know Me to know Me! Reveal Me so they will know My heart, My ways and kingdom! My deep is greatly pleased with your deep, do not give up! Your pain is producing a pressure in you that produces the flow of My Love and power in and through you in a greater measure!" Your Living Redeemer

"I did it all so you could have it all! I gave my life so you could live in my resurrection power! I am alive forever more, and I am active on the scene of your rescue! I go before you, keep your eyes on my eyes and know the power of your strength is in my redemptive blood, it is your life and breath! When our Father sees you, He sees my finished sacrifice, it is already finished, the victory has already been won! I took the keys to hell and death and overcame every enemy set against your soul and nation! Keep your eyes on the prize, the mark of your high calling, it's in Me and through Me as I live in and through you, My love! "The Precious Lamb of God

"I AM not far off! I have never left you or forsaken you! I AM your BREATH, I AM your HEARTBEAT, I AM your COMPASSION, I AM your POWER, I AM your DOMINION, I AM your AUTHORITY, I AM your

PRINCE OF PEACE, I AM your WAYMAKER, I AM for you, I AM in you,
your HOPE OF GLORY, I AM all around you! I AM NOT going to fail YOU!" The Great I AM, Your Father, the Son and Holy Spirit

"Where two or more of you agree as touching anything on earth it shall be done! The enemy hates you and is called the destroyer. I have come that you would have life and life more abundantly! Do not look at the wind and waves, only look at Me and hold on to me in agreement! Do not question in fear my power or will, fear not, only believe, my Child! You have read, even as Peter looked only on my face of love and Resurrection power and not at the circumstances, he then walked supernaturally on the waves of destruction! The enemy is under your feet, tread upon his head and look up!! Your redemption is near!! Praise and release my power and breath and spirit on the earth, I've got you!" Your Living Redeemer

"Remember who I AM! Remember I AM for you!! Who could be against you?! Remember every altar you built in thanksgiving, remembering my miraculous intervention in your life and those you love! At the same place the enemy wanted to destroy you, you worshiped with thanksgiving KNOWING I would not fail you or let you down! Remember I AM the same yesterday, today, and forever! Remember my love for you and power intervened faithfully on you and your people!

Remember I did it all for you so you could have it all, all love, power, and dominion! Guard your heart and mind and never confuse me with the enemy set to destroy your soul! Remember I Am a good father, ask for bread and I will not give you a snake, ask for an egg and I will not give you a scorpion! I gave my best so you could live and have life more abundantly!!" Abba

"When I said Follow Me and I will make you fishers of men, you followed! When I said take up your cross and follow me, the way, the truth, the life, you followed! I say to you, rise and follow me in resurrection power! I am alive, I have conquered death, hell, and every demonic force that was set against you! Keep your eyes on Me, I am not of this world. I am the resurrection and the life and am alive in and through you! Have no fear, only believe, I will not fail you, My love!!!" Your Living Redeemer

"Even as the wind blows and you can't see it, but you see the effects of my land's banner lifting and flowing in freedom as the wind sails. So is your life, your family, and your very heart as I breathe and blow the breath of my Holy Spirit in you and those you love. Faith is a substance like the wind of my spirit, not seen until you see the manifestation of the evidence that I am leading you and keeping you in the very life and vein next to my heart, the life flow of my Resurrected Son, My love! Hold on and don't let go of my word and you will see the effect of it in full manifestation. I AM for you, with you, through you, in you!" Abba

"The only way to really live and breathe and move in Me is to see Me! See my burning love for you, My love, know the sacrifice I made to call you My own! See only My plan, see only My heart for you of Love! I am love, I don't only feel love, I don't only give love. I am Love and I am for you! Rise above the status quo and the mundane and average. Rise into my supernatural realm of believing and seeing, seeing my heart, plan, and purpose in this hour! I am coming soon, for a bride that is burning for Me! Fan the flame and stir up the gifts you have received, speak my living word, manifest My power, spark up my life and spirit among My people! You are in this world, but never forget you are not of this world! Rise on the wind of My spirit and burn with passion for My way of doing things. I will not fail you!" The Lord of Hosts

"We are the perfect fit, what was not perfect is forming into my perfect will generated by my perfect love. I chose you; you did not choose me; I will not let go! I am yours and you are mine, I am forming you into my image, and nothing will separate you from my love and care! You belong, you belong to me forever, my love! We are the perfect fit!" Your Prince of Peace

"My kingdom is within your reach! I am not far off; I am right where you need me to be. I am your sustenance, the air in your lungs, the one that satisfies your soul! Your very present help in trouble, your strong hand of deliverance, the laughter and joy of your strength. Do not look to the right or to the left, keep a steady gaze on me and keep your peace still. I am with you, for you, and will not fail you! Launch out, I will exceed your greatest expectations!" says the Lord.

CPSIA information can be obtained
at www.ICGtesting.com
Printed in the USA
LVHW050740150323
741651LV00002B/47